OTHER BOOKS BY JD CROWE

Smell the Love (2007)

2005 Hurricane Season:
A graphic documentary featuring the Katrina cartoons (2006)

Dark Side of the MoonPie (2003)

Daze of Glory:
Images of Fact and Fantasy Inspired by the Gulf War (1991)

HALF-THUNK THOUGHTS
& HALF-FAST DRAWINGS

For ALAN,
Hope you GET A few
HALF-thunk Chuckles out th
this HALF-fast book.
You MIGHT FIND A FUN THING
OR 2 on PAGE 71.
Cheers!

HALF-THUNK THOUGHTS
& HALF-FAST DRAWINGS

JD CROWE

RIVER'S EDGE
——— MEDIA ———
Little Rock, Arkansas
2014

HALF-THUNK THOUGHTS AND HALF-FAST DRAWINGS

www.RiversEdgeMedia.com

Published by River's Edge Media, LLC
100 Morgan Keegan Drive, Ste. 305
Little Rock, AR 72202

Manufactured in the United States of America.

ISBN-13: 978-1-940595-16-0

For my dearly departed Mom and Pop, Dorothy and James H. Crowe.
Thanks for sharpening my pencils and supplying me with paper, pigs
and plenty of things to ponder.

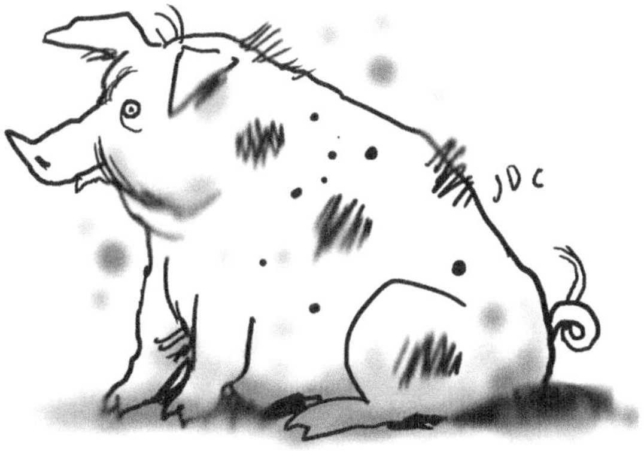
JDC

THUMB-SUCKING, DRAWING, PIGS AND TWITTER

PROLOGUE

I was a bad thumb sucker, as my mama put it. But the one thing I liked better than my thumb was a pencil. At the age of two, I could draw Roy Rogers and Trigger better than I could say their names.

As long as I was drawing, I wasn't sucking that sinful thumb.

Early on, my mama found the keys to keeping her toddler content was a grocery sack and a pencil. She would tear down a large brown paper sack and lay it out flat on the kitchen floor. I would lie there with it for a minute, gazing at its awesome emptiness, then—pencil in hand—disappear into it for hours. Mom could then go about her daily routines without a worry about me.

I only came up for air when my pencil needed sharpening. I didn't have to say a word. I just held my pencil up and Mom came swooping in with her paring knife, the one that looked a hundred years old. She laid the pencil on her left index finger and scraped the lead until the point was sharp and her fingertip was black.

My mom was the best pencil sharpener I ever saw. Each point was a work of art. And like fingerprints, no two were exactly alike.

The same knife that peeled, sliced and cut thousands of potatoes, tomatoes, apples, green beans and cantaloupes also sharpened several hundred grubby, snotty toddler pencils. Please, not a word about this to the Health Department.

Finally, with both sides of the brown sack covered in drawings, I came out of the trance and stood over the tangle of characters, lines and shapes to look at them for the first time from some distance.

Drawing is like other forms of art, sports and murder. In the zone, you don't remember the act of doing it. You emerge from the deed and there it is. You've got the pencil or the brush or the baseball bat or the shovel in your hand, so you get the blame. My crime scenes were riddled with pigs, horses, cowboys and Indians, super heroes and some ambiguous, fleshy figures good Christian people might find disturbing.

My early toddler drawings prompted the phrase my dear mother often uttered when looking at my work throughout my career: "I'm not sure what it is but I can tell it's real good."

When I wasn't on the kitchen floor carving picture stories onto torn-flat grocery sacks, I could be found hunkered down at the hog lot watching the pigs eat. Be careful out there, kids. Turns out, pondering swine and drawing can lead to a life of political cartooning.

I've never cared much for politicians, but when you nail one with a cartoon it's great fun to hear 'em squeal. I've been in the business of drawing editorial cartoons for over 30 years now.

There's never a lack of material, especially in the South. But occasionally, politics makes my brain hurt. Alabama is a target-rich environment where the politicians never tire of spinning their own satire, but it gets tiresome playing Whack-a-mole at their shenanigans.

Sometimes, I like to draw stuff just for the fun of it—without thinking too much. That's where this book comes in.

A few years ago, I discovered Twitter and stumbled upon a

coven of tweeters who were writing random stupid stuff that was laugh-out-loud funny.

"These are my Tweeple," I half-thought out loud to myself.

So I jumped on the hamster wheel and started writing my own random stupid stuff. Brevity is the soul of wit, and at 140 characters a pop, brevity is mandatory on Twitter. It became a fun writing tool, and I enjoyed this fast, whimsical new playground.

So, what do you do with a pile of half-thunk thoughts? If you're a cartoonist, you draw some of them and put 'em in a book.

I hope you enjoy reading these *Half-thunk Thoughts and Half-fast Drawings* as much as I enjoyed half-thinking them. If you read one you like, tell somebody about it. Because here's the real reason for publishing this stuff:

"I just wanna be quoted."

– Me

Follow J.D. Crowe on Facebook and on Twitter from @Crowejam and @Crowetoons.

Go to AL.com for J.D.'s daily editorial cartoons and commentary.

A cartoonist should be obscene
and not heard.

Where I come from,
a man will look into the distance
and think for a spell.
And then he'll spit.

Don't mess with him
before he spits.

The men in my family don't like
to talk about our underwear.

We're the thong
silent type.

Where I come from,
"stock options" is
a farm animal dating site.

Sighs matter.

My favorite people are the ones
who suffer in silence.

Where I come from,
reading anything out loud
is considered
showin' off.

I am a recovering redneck.
It's been three weeks since
I dry humped a cousin.

I don't know why we always schedule
our family reunion
during cousin mating season.

4 out of my 5 teeth
can't recommend a good
dentist.

Where I come from,
makeup sex is what happens
when the Avon Lady gets drunk
with the rodeo clown.

I was raised redneck
and I'm half lesbian on my mama's side.
So yeah, I'm comfortable in flannel.

I had a mouth-breathin' cousin
who drowned while gettin' baptized
but that's OK at least he was saved.

Not to brag, but if a bomb
hit this Walmart right now, my body
might be the only one identified.
I have dental records.

This woman in Walmart has a
lovely set of March Madness teeth.
She's down to the final four.

Afraid if I cut my mullet off
I won't be taken seriously
as an air guitarist.

Redneck inbreeding:
Real. Comfortable.
Genes.

The
tragic
irony is,
I thought the mullet
was hiding
my red
neck.

This mullet's like a lizard's tail. I cut it
off, but it grows right back
as soon as I walk into Walmart.

Not to brag, but I still fit
into the same wife beater
I wore at my wedding.

Grow 'em long, men.
Even the mangiest mullet will some day
make a dandy combover.

The back-to-front comb over:
Where mullets are laid to rest.

Just saw a tractor trailer on its side
nursing a litter of smart cars.

The Snuggie is a gateway garment
to the burqa.

Wonder if the Pope and KKK ever run
into each other at the laundromat?

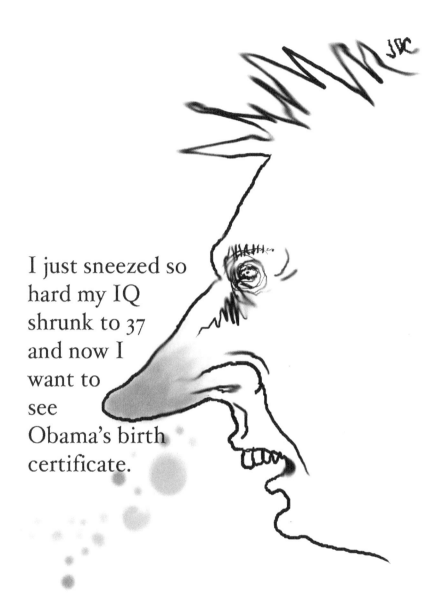

I just sneezed so hard my IQ shrunk to 37 and now I want to see Obama's birth certificate.

I'm no doctor, but some of the women
I saw in Walmart have
a very bad case of babies.

Just sneezed so hard
I pollinated a meadow of lesbians.

I'm not into redneck gay porn
or anything, but one time at the county
fair I got my prostate checked
while eating a corn dog.

If your idea of a good time involves a corn dog, a 6-pack and a corpse, you **might** be a redneck-ro-philiac.

Where I come from,
"scaring up something to eat"
is an invitation to supper.

Give a man a fish, no problem.
Give a man the finger, he'll get all
huffy and wrestle you
out of his boat.

You can be anything you want
as long as you grow up to be the
same as everyone else.

I just found my imaginary life
remote control.
This changes everything.

Be the change
you're looking for between
the couch cushions.

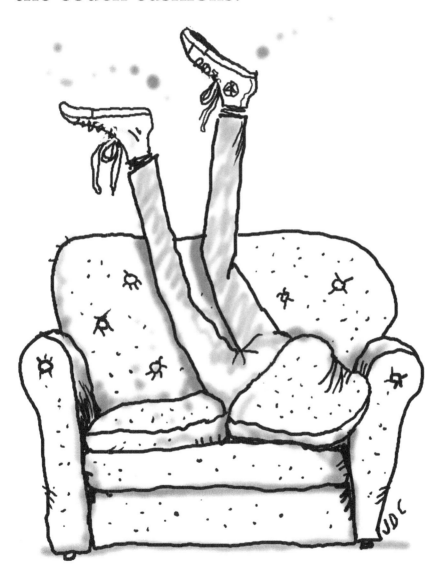

I am the Shaun White
of Extreme sliding around the house
in my footie pajamas.

My Indian stripper name
is Dances With Daddy Issues.

Never judge a man until
you skip a while
in his footie
pajamas.

Where I come from, 'uncoupling'
is what you do to 2 dogs
with a water hose.

An older woman in an animal print
mini skirt knocked on my door
and so anyway I think I just bought
some Cougar Scout cookies.

Sane as it never was.

That's the last time
I play Twister with a
guy in a
kilt.

Worst part about raising a garden
is trying to keep the cougars
off the cucumbers.

There's a bald spot in my yard
so I'm gonna let the grass around it
grow really long and then
do a comb-over.

You can't swing a dead cat on this porch
without hitting the neighbor in the face
with some terrible news
about her cat.

I use my best
Greco-Roman wrestling moves
every time I engage
a folding
lawn chair.

Curling is just housework on ice.

My least favorite Olympic event is
the men's figure dating.

Looking forward to watching some of
that synchronized sinning.

My bid to win a medal in speed skating was hampered by my mom, who packed only my bowling shoes.

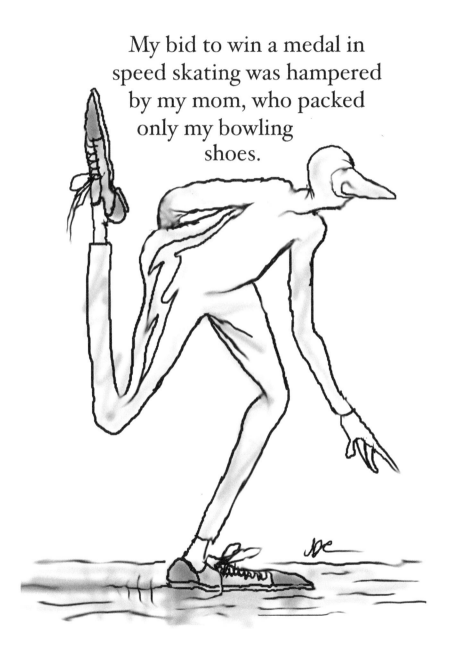

Never had a conversation I couldn't turn into a Freudian slip n' slide.

I walk the streets in constant fear of tripping and accidentally humping a hobo.

Regrets? I got a Brazilian.

One thing led to another and now
I'm in a hotel room with the
TSA screener, having a cigarette
and pondering my
daddy issues.

I like to play church with small animals.
Today I'm baptizing hamsters and
tomorrow I'll be preaching
their little funerals.

Time to harvest the shower drain.
Any o' you kids want a hamster?

Q: Are hamsters bred?

A: No.
Biscuits are bread.
Hamsters are furry
lunch meat.

"Men, we need a durable lunch meat
that can also be used as a hockey puck."
— Makers of Spam

Named my hamster Spam
so when he dies I can bury
him in a little tin coffin
with his name on it.

Uncle Harry had a hamster
He taught to sit and stay
He put it on his shiny head
and wore it as a toupee

One day the hamster hairpiece
Got the urge to stray
It slid down to Harry's lip
And happily humped away

Harry pulled the beast from
his face and spanked its little
butt
"Sorry to admit," the uncle spit
"My mustache is such a slut."

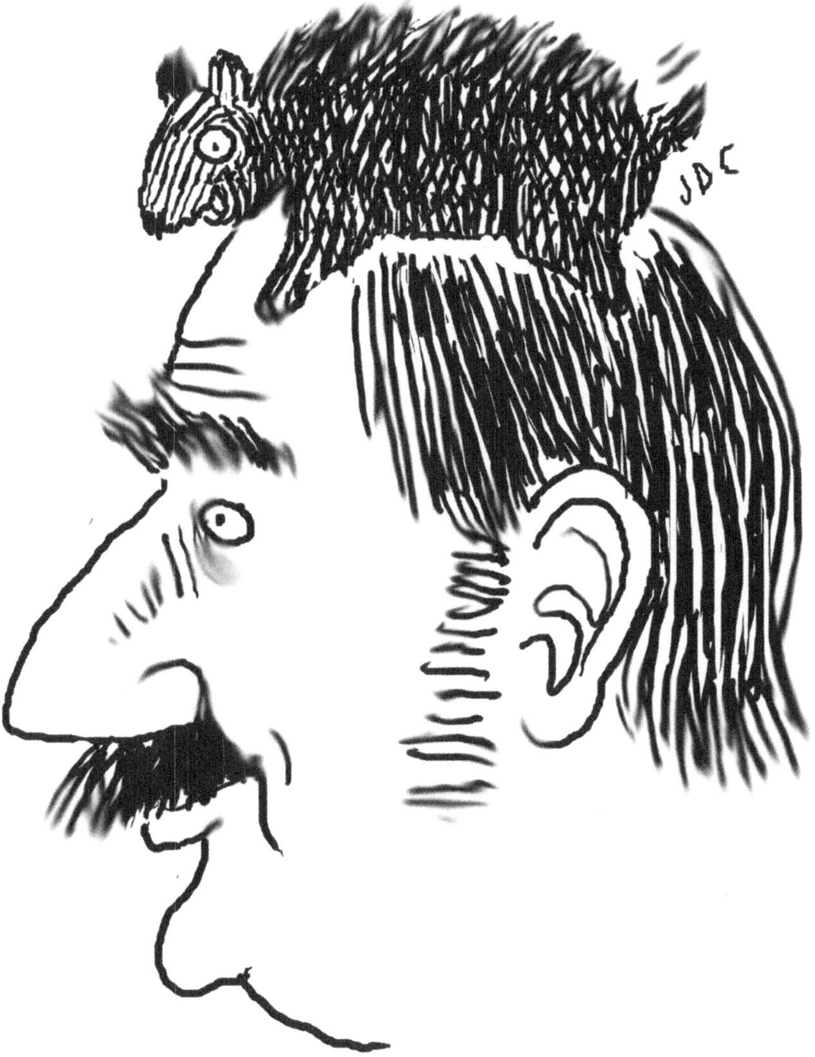
JDC

Stop faking sense.

I taught my hamster
everything it needed
to know about bowling.

Except for that part about
"letting go."

I never know what to do with my arms
when I'm sleeping, dancing
or talking to an Italian.

I hate weddings, funerals
and the symphony.
I never know when to clap.

I'm uncomfortable talking about
anything I know something about.

Don't give a man a fish
and then give him the finger
or he'll slap you in the face
with that fish.

Proud to live in a country
where troubled inner city youths
have hope of some day
banging a Kardashian.

Tried to help my daughter
with a science project
but wound up making a big meth.

Did a splendid face plant
into the kitty litter box
and the dog and I are sharing
a laugh and a cigar.

Droopy drawers
are the
gateway
to
crack.

Tired of being fat and pasty?
Put tanning bed lights
in your refrigerator.

If you post a pic of what you're
about to eat, please post a pic of
the poop that follows. We're dying
to see how the story ends.

The dog just looked right through me
like he saw my soul
or maybe the baloney slices
I'm hiding in my shirt.

Tossed and turned all night.
I gotta stop using
salad dressing as
a moisturizer.

I put a lot of pressure on myself
to act all nonchalant.

My favorite unthinkable thoughts
are the ones that never get thunk.

If I wasn't so deprived
I wouldn't be so depraved.

I have no one to blame
but my elf.

My signature move is something I call
the "flinch and grimace."

I cling to my schizophrenia because
I'm afraid to be alone with my thoughts.

I fear I'm not as paranoid as I should be.

My comfort zone
is a miserable little
place.

People are the worst, but not the imaginary ones. You guys are cool.

Starting to think the guy who's been sleeping on my couch isn't the real Kurt Cobain.

Tell me, where is this "comfort zone" you speak of?

Personal space office tip:
People tend to give you plenty
of room when you make
tractor noises.

I'm as affectionate as the next guy.
(Great. Now the next guy
wants to spoon.)

Stop squirming!
I'm trying to read your body language.

I have the same problem
with man hugs that I do
with bowling.
I never know when
to let go.

Let's pretend one of us never happened.

I can tell how uncomfortable
a person is just by
hugging them for
17 minutes.

I wear a cape when I'm driving
so if I get pulled over the cop will think
I'm going somewhere to fight crime.

It's important to use lots of
ambiguloquacious words so people
won't know what you're trying
to trick them into thinking.

I took a vowel of pverty.

If you have a nemesis
at work, you should wear a cape
so people will know
you're the
good guy.

In hindsight, I think this wedgie
is obstructing my vision.

Not sure why my butt feels weird but
I think a ventriloquist had a hand in it.

I ran into my proctologist and his wife
in public and he pretended not to know
me and now I'm feeling kinda
hurt and slutty.

The worst part
about fighting crime:
Cape wedgies.

We're all circling the drain,
but some of us are getting sucked
into it louder than others.

Nothing funnier
than painful childhood memories.

The worst part of the
super hero's very bad day began
when the arch enemy saw my cape
sticking out of the
porta-potty.

I trust you but I don't
turn my back on you trust you.

Keep your friends nervous
and your enemies guessing.

I miss you but it's more
of a take-a-swing-at-and-miss you.

Give a man a fish, everything's cool.
But give that man the finger and he'll
chase you down the stairwell
and make a big scene
here at work.

Under a bridge, harassing goats.
That's how I troll.

My November facial hair doesn't say
"Hollywood chic" as much as it whispers
"soup kitchen creepy."

Sleep like nobody's watching.
Go ahead. I haven't got all night.

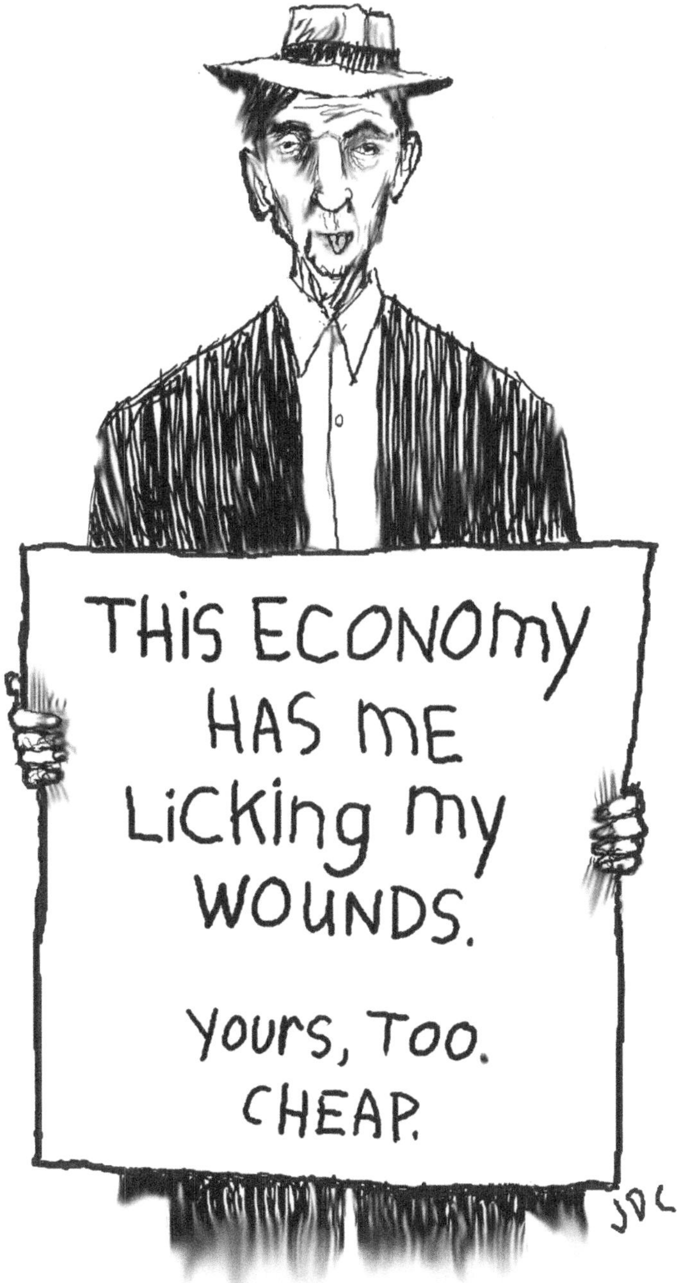
THIS ECONOMY HAS ME LICKING MY WOUNDS.
YOURS, TOO. CHEAP.
JDC

Sex is like riding a bike.
If you do it on a busy street
you should at least wear
a helmet.

Sex with altar boys?
Nun for me, thanks.

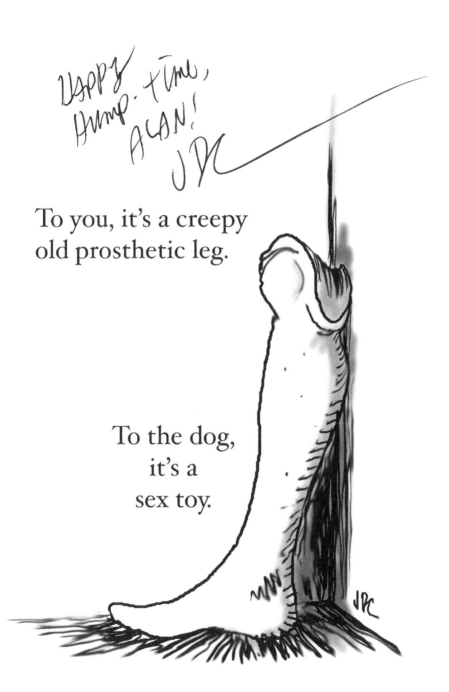

To you, it's a creepy
old prosthetic leg.

To the dog,
it's a
sex toy.

Smart, beautiful women
give me the confidence and vocabulary
of a drunken toddler.

Men, always jingle the change
in your pockets really loud
so the ladies will know
you got it goin' on down there.

When life hands you women,
make women laid.

If I knew then
what I know now,
I would have been a really creepy,
sexually frustrated
toddler.

Giving blood today.
Not my own, of course.
That would be creepy.

Doctor says my habit of urinating
under random bridges puts me at high
risk for a run-in with Gary Busey.

My favorite babies are the ones who flash
an evil grin moments before someone
bursts into flames.

I'm going
through that
awkward stage
between
creepy young
guy and
creepy dead
guy.

It's not the feat,
it's the futility.

She blinded me with silence.

I can walk up to any dog,
rub its butt and make a friend for life.
That trick only works
about half the time
on people.

"I'd hit that if I was drunk."

- Me, driving by a mailbox
just now

Reports of my breath
have been greatly inebriated.

I'm in no condition to thrive.

If you have a good dog,
you don't really need a gun,
an ottoman, a dishwasher
or a bidet.

I am better off now
than I was four
beers ago.

If you can't laugh at yourself, that's ok.
You're providing plenty of material
for the rest of us.

I only tweet when I have nothing to say.

Lime flies when you're having rum

JDC

I'd settle for separation
of church and snakes.

I am comfortable in my own sin.

Starting a new religion
and the only sinners are people
who take things literally.

Bent over to pick up a
stick and the stick
moved and oh yeah
so did my
bowels

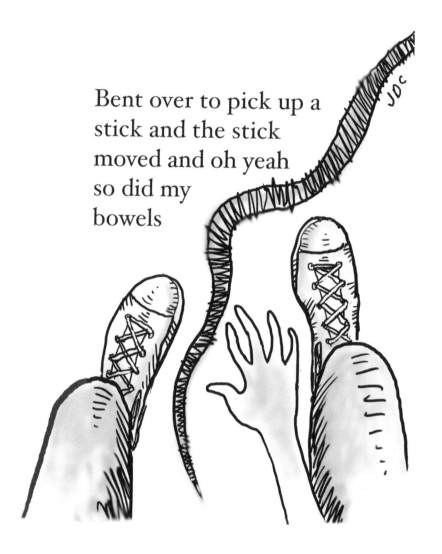

In the South, any time you wander
too close to a river
you're in danger of being baptized.

Truth is, I was raised Baptist.
Lynyrd Skynyrd Baptist,
not Westboro Baptist.

True friends stick with you
through sick and sin.

You can tell pretty quickly
how evil a person is
by how much they resist
being
surprise-baptized.

Having a small, quiet family dinner
for Thanksgiving.
Small, quiet families are easier to eat
than large loud ones.

Well, these vegans aren't
gonna eat themselves.

"You say cousin, I say cuisine."
— A snooty cannibal.

Get a grip, heathens.
These snakes ain't
gonna handle
themselves.

"Forgive me dude, for I have thinned."
—My hair

Zombies are just looking
for a little piece of mind.

Angels are just dead people
who drink Red Bull.

Let him who
is without skin cast
the first bone.

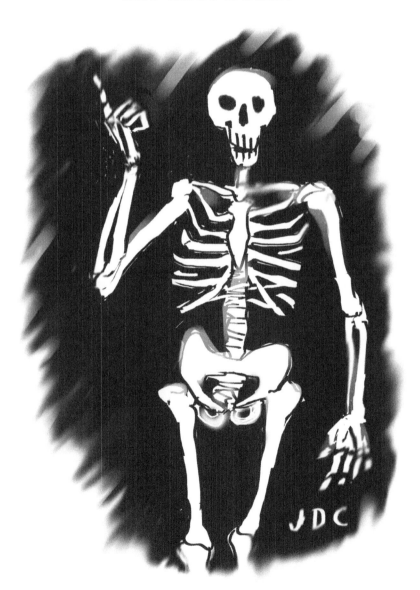

Wish there was a place where we could write random nonsense just to see if any little imaginary people would react to it.

We're just a room full of monkeys and Twitter is our typewriter.

I hate being cut down to sighs.

Writing a novel about
small rodents in the South.
calling it:
'Of Mice and Mullets'

Children are our greatest
natural resource,
so let's put the fat bastards on treadmills
and hook 'em up to the power grid.

I like toddlers the way I like my lobsters.
Taken out of the restaurant and turned
loose in the woods.

The hardest part about doing a Nativity
scene is teaching the baby to Tebow.

Doing my part to fight childhood obesity
by chasing fat toddlers into traffic.

This Play-doh
tastes like filthy
children
fingers.

Inside every homophobe is a pouty
princess longing for a coming-out party.

You can pretty much weed out the
homophobes at the gym by calling
for a group hug in the showers.

They pray away the gay, then wait
to be straight? It's intense to be dense.

This day has taken more turns
than a homophobe
walking the streets of
San Francisco.

If I ever have sex with a man
I really, really hope it's with a gay guy
because at least one of us
should know what
to do.

If you're a gay man in a straitjacket,
I'm sorry. You just can't pull it off.

If I ever
turn
gay

I'm afraid
I won't be able
to keep a
straight face.

That time you turned the corner
and ran into me and I said
'Shall we dance?' and we laughed
—I planned that for like 6 months.

You strike me as a person
who likes to hit people.

If I make you mad it's just because
I'm trying to get in your rants.

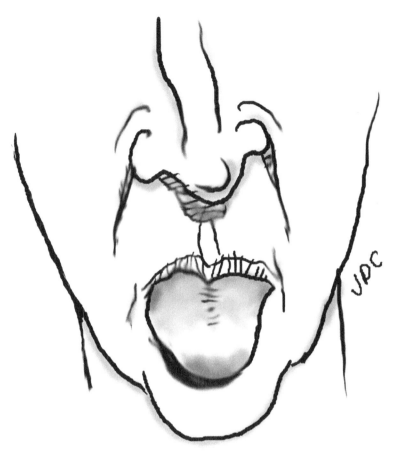

The most humiliating
unnatural act I perform is
when I'm forced to be
the adult in the
relationship.

Marriage is an out-of-booty experience.

Told her I'd rather eat laundry
than fold it and now I'm having
boxers for breakfast.

I'm too immature for adultery.

When wife hands you lemons,
don't make a stupid joke about
how you prefer melons
or you will end up holding
your banana.

My wife asked me
what I was thinking about
so I played dead and now she's
dating a guy she met
at my funeral.

My man cave has wife-eye.

Hell hath no fury like a woman
rearranging furniture.

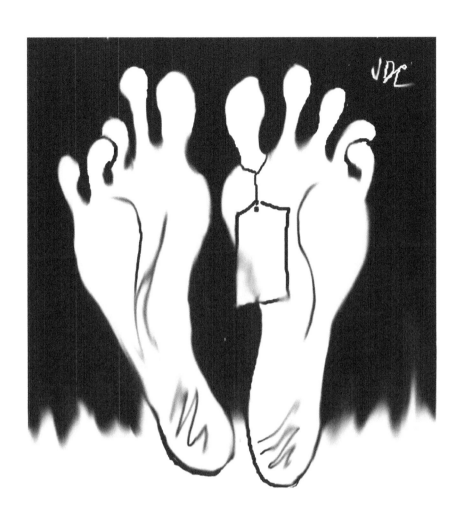

My wife's favorite position
is the one where I lie very still
wearing nothing but a toe tag
and she starts dating again.

She's so far out of my league
she's playing for the other team.

My dog just told me he's been
faking his leg thumps.

I'll believe corporations are people
when conservatives ban them
from marrying each other.

It's gotten to where my leg goes to
sleep as soon as the dog starts
humping it.

It's like they're married.

Some people would rather eat dirt
than find common ground.

If I ever do anything I'm really proud of
I'll probably have to spend
the rest of my life apologizing for it.

Show me a deaf husband
and I'll show you
evidence of a
merciful
God.

Where I come from,
farm animals are:
1. Pets 2. Dates 3. Dinner

I'd rather eat ZZ Top's beards
and drink Willie Nelson's bong water
than see another goober
Texas governor as president.

Wanna hook a fish?
····   Give him a cigarette.

Punxsutawney Phil came out
of the closet and is now having angry sex
with that thing on Donald Trump's head.

Those Tea Party people are gonna
be mad at Donald Trump when they find
out that thing on his head
has been killing their chickens.

Sometimes the pitch
of Sarah Palin's voice is so high
the only one who can hear it
is that thing on Donald Trump's head.

Late at night,
that thing on Donald Trump's
head sneaks out of the house
and has angry sex with
possums.

Twerk like nobody's retching.

I think my blow-up doll is cheating on me with the inflatable pool boy.

Truth is,
I don't have the cajones
to be a diva like Madonna.
Cajones are those pointy
bra things, right?

Steve Buscemi is proof
that Don Knotts banged a cat.

Any time someone besides me reaches
for the check at a restaurant I act like
Taylor Swift when she wins an award.

"That Steve Buscemi is a good looking guy."

- John Waters

When tickled by the feather of truth,
the guilty will bellow as if
bludgeoned by
a hammer.

Sometimes, living the dream simply
means surviving a nightmare.

If I ever meet Kathy Bates
I will say, "Hobbled to meet you."
And then I think we will
wrestle.

You never get a second chance
to make a good fist impression.

As they say in Florida,
any day you wake up
and you weren't swallowed whole
by the earth while you were sleeping
is a good day.

Mardi Gras was a mess.
Ain't seen so much cheap jewelry flyin'
around since a tornado hit
the redneck mafia trailer park.

I'm white,
but I'm not
Betty
White.

You know you're right
when the right people
think you're wrong.

Worst part about sleeping with a mime
is watching 'em snore all night.

Never underestimate
a man's passion for apathy.

I'll have the blackened soul.

"Debt man walking."
—My creditors, talking trash

I see debt people.

Even at death's door,
I will remain a Southern
gentleman and insist
that you go
first.

I love to clutch my chest and
gasp for breath so one day
people can say
"at least he died doing what he loved."

Funerals are more fun when you prop
the corpse up in a kissing booth.

Nobody has more fun at work
than a mortician/ventriloquist.

At my funeral I will sit on a guy's lap telling jokes for an hour and then the mortician/ventriloquist will stick me in a suitcase.

Not to brag, but I can still wear
the same suit I was buried in.

Just bought a used death bed and now
I've got buyer's rigor mortis.

If death turns out
to be a surprise party
I'm gonna **hate** the
part where dead people
in little hats
jump out at me.

I'm too shallow for this grave.

Went to bed dead and woke up
with mourning breath.

So, anybody wanna buy
a slightly used death bed?

If I ever have a funeral
I hope it's the kind where
I jump out and scare my friends
to death because I'm
afraid to die alone.

Woke up in a graveyard.
Never felt more alive.

I'm not the creepiest guy in this coffin.

I just woke up
and scared the hell out of this
mortician.

"I just wanna be quoted."
— Me

ABOUT THE AUTHOR

JD Crowe grew up on a farm in Kentucky where he
raised pigs, tobacco and, according to photos,
a pretty good mullet.

JD is now the statewide cartoonist for Alabama Media Group.
His cartoons and essays appear daily on Al.com and in print in
The Birmingham News, Mobile Press-Register and The Huntsville
Times.

JD has illustrated and published several books of his work,
and his twisted/folksy humor makes him a popular speaker
all along the Gulf Coast.

JD lives in Fairhope, Alabama, with his wife, daughter and
several furry critters.

CPSIA information can be obtained at www.ICGtesting.com
Printed in the USA
LVOW05s1926181214

419052LV00002BA/2/P